ROALD DAHL

SCRUMPTIOUS & DELUMPTIOUS

WORDS

Original text by
Roald Dahl

Illustrated by
Quentin Blake

Compiled by
Kay Woodward

OXFORD
UNIVERSITY PRESS

MMM...

Some words can make your mouth water, just by reading them. Others can make you screw up your face so much that you look as if you just sucked a bagful of lemons. Roald Dahl **LOVED** food and his books are peppered with a great many lip-smackingly glorious words (and downright yucksome words, too). He even invented a few of his own.

Wouldn't it be fabulous if these **scrumptious** and **delumptious** words were collected together in one handy book? Well, guess what . . . they are! And, even better, this is that book! We have harvested these truly toothsome words from Roald Dahl's stories, so you don't have to. There are handy tips for making your own writing terrifically tasty too.

But before you go any further, here is a very important warning: **NEVER read this book when you are even a tiny bit hungry.** This is guaranteed to make your stomach growl louder than the angriest giant. And then you won't be able to hear yourself think. Or read.

— Kay Woodward

CONTENTS

FANTASTIC feasts

Are you bored of bolognaise? Do you long for a meal that is larger than life? And would you like to share this marvellous meal with all of your favourite people? Then what YOU need is a feast like this.

*The **feast** was just beginning. A lar[ge] dining-room had been hollowed ou[t] of the earth, and in the middle of it, seated around a huge table, were n[o] less than twenty-nine animals . . .*

— FANTASTIC MR FOX

feast *noun*

A *feast* is a grand meal, usually for many people . . .
or foxes, of course. It's a way of celebrating a special
occasion, such as a birthday, a festival or a glorious victory
over three dastardly farmers. There's always *oodles* of
scrumdiddlyumptious food.

feast or famine

This is a phrase that means there is either too much of
something or too little. To a fox, a huge shed teeming with
chickens is *definitely* a feast.

phizz-whizzing foodie fact

A meal that you enjoy with friends in the middle
of the night is called a **midnight feast**. They are
usually eaten in secret, because grown-ups don't
approve of that sort of thing. (Spoilsports.)

You don't have to eat a feast at a table, sitting bolt upright, using a napkin and using eleven different knives, forks and spoons. Feasts can take place on a picnic rug, at the beach, in a treehouse or in a gazillion other places. In fact, you can **GOLLOP** a feast just about ANYWHERE.

gollop *verb*

To gollop means to swallow food hastily or greedily.
The word, which dates back to the early 19th century,
may perhaps be a mixture of **gulp** and **gobble**.

Augustus Gloop's feast takes place somewhere quite
extraordinary – on the bank of a chocolate river, which is
flowing with hot melted chocolate of the highest quality.
(WARNING: this type of feast is absolutely **NOT ALLOWED**.
Just ask Willy Wonka.)

*Augustus Gloop, as you might have guessed, had quietly
sneaked down to the edge of the river, and he was now
kneeling on the riverbank, scooping hot melted chocolate
into his mouth as fast as he could.*

— CHARLIE AND THE CHOCOLATE FACTORY

9

ONOMATOPOEIC (*say on-o-mat-o-pee-ik*) words sound like the thing they describe. Many of the different verbs Roald Dahl used to describe eating are **ONOMATOPOEIC**.

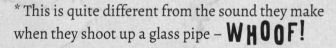

nibble   suck   gulp   wolf   chew   gobble   guzzle   nosh   chomp   munch   slurp

Can you think of any more examples? To reveal whether a word is **ONOMATOPOEIC** or not, try saying it aloud.

Augustus Gloop's surname could be **ONOMATOPOEIC** too. It sounds rather like the noise a boy might make when he falls into a melted chocolate river. **GLOOP!***

* This is quite different from the sound they make when they shoot up a glass pipe – **WHOOF!**

10

The word *feast* is super handy. It isn't just a noun.
It can also be used as a **verb**.

feast *verb*

To feast means to dine on **delumptious** food until all you
can do is sigh happily, pat your tummy and say, 'I'm as full
as an egg'. And if you have ever cracked an egg, you'll know
that they are Very Full Indeed.

*Augustus Gloop! Augustus Gloop! / The great big
greedy nincompoop! / How long could we allow this
beast / To gorge and guzzle, feed and feast . . .*
— CHARLIE AND THE CHOCOLATE FACTORY

In Roald Dahl's stories, his characters feast on all sorts of **wondercrump** dishes in both spectacular and tediously dull places. The BFG eats an enormous breakfast in the Great Ballroom of Buckingham Palace. The Wormwoods just eat in front of the telly. (Gosh, what an idea!)

The suppers were TV dinners in floppy aluminium containers with separate compartments for the stewed meat, the boiled potatoes and the peas.

— MATILDA

The BFG grabbed the garden spade and scooped up all the eggs, sausages, bacon and potatoes in one go and shovelled them into his enormous mouth.
'By goggles!' he cried. 'This stuff is making snozzcumbers taste like swatchwallop!'

— THE BFG

Meanwhile, Mr Twit can eat **ANYWHERE**. He feasts all day long on leftover food that has been festering in his dirty old beard for months and months.

. . . Mr Twit never went really hungry. By sticking out his tongue and curling it sideways to explore the hairy jungle around his mouth, he was always able to find a tasty morsel here and there to nibble on.

— THE TWITS

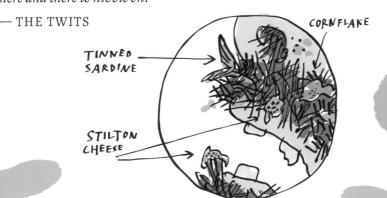

CORNFLAKE

TINNED SARDINE

STILTON CHEESE

If you could choose any food in the world, what would YOU feast upon?

'I look and smell,' Aunt Sponge declared,
'as lovely as a rose! Just feast your eyes
upon my face, observe my shapely nose!'
— JAMES AND THE GIANT PEACH

Aunt Sponge doesn't really want Aunt Spiker's
eyes to eat her. That would be **redunculous**. 'Feast
your eyes' is an **idiom**. This is a phrase that means
something more than the simple meaning of
the words. For example, 'feast your eyes' actually
means 'gaze with pleasure'. So, would you like to
feast your eyes upon Aunt Sponge . . . ?

Here are more scrumptious idioms and their meanings.

The big cheese

– a super important person, such as someone in charge of a company

Not my cup of tea

– when something isn't the sort of thing you like

A piece of cake

– when something is very, very easy to do

To go bananas

– to become very, very overexcited

As cool as a cucumber

– when someone is super relaxed

To spill the beans

– to reveal secret information

A hot potato

– a subject that is likely to upset people. Like a hot potato, it's best to avoid touching it.

15

GORGE, gobble AND GUZZLE

Would *you* like to eat a thick slice of the Trunchbull's ginormous chocolate cake? It's made from real butter and real cream. It's covered with dark-brown chocolate icing. It's lickswishy! You would? Excellent.

But wait! You don't just have to **EAT** the cake. Instead, you could **DEVOUR** it or **GOBBLE** it or **GULP** it down. You could **SCOFF** the cake or **STUFF YOUR FACE** with it. You could make the Trunchbull really mad and **POLISH IT OFF**.

Psst! These words are all synonyms for 'eat'.

16

TORTOISE, TORTOISE,
GET BIGGER, BIGGER!
COME ON, TORTOISE,
GROW UP, PUFF UP, SHOOT UP!
SPRING UP, BLOW UP, SWELL UP!
GORGE, GUZZLE, STUFF, GULP!
PUT ON FAT, TORTOISE, PUT ON FAT!
*GET ON, GET ON, **GOBBLE** FOOD!*
— ESIO TROT

A **synonym** is a word or phrase that means exactly or nearly the same as another word or phrase. Synonyms are a genius way of turning an ordinary sentence into something truly magnificent, just by changing a word or two.

Phizz-whizzing tip

A thesaurus looks a little like a dictionary, but instead of definitions, it's full to the brim with synonyms instead. So if you'd like to find a different way of saying something, look inside!

You might even find one full of the words Roald Dahl invented!

Here are more ways of describing 'eating' that you'll find in Roald Dahl's stories.

Mrs Wormwood sat **munching** her meal with her eyes glued to the American soap-opera on the screen.

— MATILDA

*Charlie went on **wolfing** the chocolate. He couldn't stop. And in less than half a minute, the whole thing had disappeared down his throat.*

— CHARLIE AND THE CHOCOLATE FACTORY

*'At this moment,' continued the Ladybird, 'our Centipede, who has a pair of jaws as sharp as razors, is up there on top of the peach **nibbling away** at that stem.'*

— JAMES AND THE GIANT PEACH

*When the BFG had **consumed** his seventy-second fried egg, Mr Tibbs sidled up to the Queen.*

— THE BFG

*The table was covered with chickens and ducks and geese and hams and bacon, and everyone was **tucking into** the lovely food.*

— FANTASTIC MR FOX

19

FABULOUS food

'Hey!' you might cry. 'Why doesn't my local shop sell whangdoodles? Where do I find frobscottle?' Aha! The truth is that the world's greatest storyteller invented a great many of the eye-popping treats that he wrote about. And this means you won't find them anywhere. If you're looking for a snozzcumber, however, that's probably a good thing.

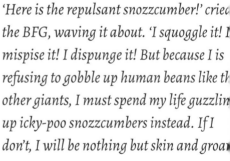

'Here is the repulsant snozzcumber!' cried the BFG, waving it about. 'I squoggle it! I mispise it! I dispunge it! But because I is refusing to gobble up human beans like th[e] other giants, I must spend my life guzzlin[g] up icky-poo snozzcumbers instead. If I don't, I will be nothing but skin and groa[n]
— THE BFG

snozzcumber noun

A snozzcumber is a knobbly vegetable that looks like a cucumber, but is much, much bigger. It is the length of one and a half men, but a great deal thicker. But before you are tempted to visit Giant Country, slice up a snozzcumber and pop it in a scrumptious salad, there is something else you should know. Snozzcumbers taste **UTTERLY DISGUSTEROUS**.

Sophie took a small nibble. 'Uggggggggh!' she spluttered. 'Oh no! Oh gosh! Oh help!' She spat it out quickly. 'It tastes of frogskins!' she gasped. 'And rotten fish!' 'Worse than that!' cried the BFG, roaring with laughter. 'To me it is tasting of clockcoaches and slime-wanglers!'

— THE BFG

A neologism (say nee-o-lo-jiz-um) is a brand new word or expression. Roald Dahl invented over 500 of them!

wonderveg *noun*
This is a delicious-tasting vegetable, or vegitibble, as the BFG calls them.

trogfilth *noun*
This is something that tastes disgusting.

Stickjaw *noun*
Willy Wonka invented this super-sticky toffee. It is so sticky and chewy that it makes your teeth stick together so that you cannot talk. (Psst. It is also the perfect way to shush talkative parents.)

*'The forest floor is safe at last for us to walk on! So now we can all go down to pick blackberries and **winkleberries** and **puckleberries** and **muckleberries** and **twinkleberries** and **snozzberries** to our heart's content.'*
— THE MINPINS

tinkle-tinkle tree *noun*

The tinkle-tinkle tree (its clever Latin-sounding name is *tinculus polyflorus*) is an exotic tree that bears pink and white blossoms. Without tinkle-tinkle flowers, there would be no Geraneous Giraffes! (Gasp.)

'I am a Geraneous Giraffe and a Geraneous Giraffe cannot eat anything except the pink and purple flowers of the tinkle-tinkle tree!'

— THE GIRAFFE AND
THE PELLY AND ME

INVENT YOUR OWN BRAND-NEW FOODIE WORDS!

1 Choose a word.

2 Think of a sound to add at the end or the beginning.

3 Stick them together.

4 If there are too many letters in the middle of the word, lose a few.

5 Ta-daaaaa!

INVENT YOUR OWN FABULOUS FRUIT OR VEGITIBBLE!

1 Write down the name of a real fruit or **vegitibble**, ideally one with a long name. For example: **SATSUMA**.

2 Cross out the first few letters of the word. Here, you will be left with **SUMA**.

3 Now make up a totally **redunculous** word. Here's one: **SQUOFFLE**.

4 Now stick the **redunculous** word at the beginning of your half-a-word. For example, this time, your new fruit would be the ... **SQUOFFLESUMA**.

5 Once you've invented your fruit or **vegitibble**, all you have to do is imagine what it tastes like ... Will it be **delumptious** or downright **repulsant**? It's up to YOU.

Sometimes, food can be made fabulous simply by making everyday items **VERY, VERY BIG INDEED.**

a peach almost as big as a house

an enormous round chocolate cake

Sometimes, there's a type of food so **HUGE**, so **CHOCOLATEY** or so **MIND-BOGGLINGLY AND UTTERLY FABULOUS** that, to describe it, only a superlative will do. This is an adjective or an adverb that expresses the highest degree of fabulousness possible.

As for James, he was so spellbound by the whole thing that he could only stand and stare and murmur quietly to himself, 'Oh, isn't it beautiful. It's the **most beautiful** thing I've ever seen.'

— JAMES AND THE GIANT PEACH

'I shall now send a bar of my **very best** chocolate from one end of this room to the other – by television! Get ready, there! Bring in the chocolate!'

Immediately, six Oompa-Loompas marched forward carrying on their shoulders the **most enormous** bar of chocolate Charlie had ever seen. It was about the size of the mattress he slept on at home.

— CHARLIE AND THE CHOCOLATE FACTORY

SUGARY, splongy OR GROBSWITCHY

Adjectives are an extraordinarily useful way of describing what food looks and tastes like. Here are just a few, but there are **dillions** and **dillions** more to choose from.

stodgy fiery
nutty
cheesy crispy bitte
sugary salty sweet
minty spicy splong
sour crumbly

Charlie put the mug to his lips, and as the rich warm creamy chocolate ran down his throat into his empty tummy, his whole body from head to toe began to tingle with pleasure.

— CHARLIE AND THE CHOCOLATE FACTORY

And they all went over to the tunnel entrance and began scooping out great chunks of juicy, golden-coloured peach flesh.

— JAMES AND THE GIANT PEACH

'It is a little bit like mixing a cake,' the BFG said. 'If you is putting . . . different things into it, you is making the cake come out any way you want, sugary, splongy, curranty, Christmassy or grobswitchy.'

— THE BFG

splongy *adjective*

A splongy mixture is both thick and springy. (It's one of the brilliant words Roald Dahl invented by joining together the words splodge and spongy – like a sponge cake.)

grobswitchy *adjective*

Something that tastes grobswitchy has a nasty flavour.

29

SMILE, IT'S A simile!

If you're tremendously hungry, then tucking into a **delumptious** meal will make you feel full and ready for anything. But did you know that food doesn't *just* give you energy and vitamins and wotnot? It can be used to add flavour to descriptions too!

Phizz-whizzing tip

A **simile** is a phrase that describes something in a vivid way; it does this by comparing it with another thing that is very, very different. Similes are easy to recognize because they use the word 'as' or 'like'.

30

That face of hers . . . was so crumpled and wizened, so shrunken and shrivelled, it looked as though it had been pickled in vinegar.

— THE WITCHES

Mrs Salt . . . was now kneeling right on the edge of the hole with her head down and her enormous behind sticking up in the air like a giant mushroom.

— CHARLIE AND THE CHOCOLATE FACTORY

One half of the Earthworm, looking like a great, thick, juicy, pink sausage, lay innocently in the sun for all the seagulls to see.

— JAMES AND THE GIANT PEACH

Would you like to make readers say, '**GOSH!**
What an unusual way to describe something, but how
brilliant and clever. I can picture it now!'? Then you
need a simile. Practise by describing someone's face.

1 Pick a face to describe. This can belong to a real
person or someone totally made-up.

2 Choose a facial feature. It could be a nose or
eyebrows or a mouth or ears – anything you like!

3 Now imagine all the totally random foods that the face
feature could look even a little bit like. If it's a nose,
does it look like a pickled onion or a wedge of cheese?
Are the cheeks as purple as pomegranates or as pale as
porridge? Let your imagination **GO WILD**.

PICK ONE OF THESE . . .

Ears

Chin

Nose

Cheeks

Eyebrows

Eyes

. . . AND PAIR IT WITH ONE OF THESE!

. . . like a **giant** mushroom

. . . like a **great**, **thick**, **juicy**, pink sausage

. . . that looked as though it had been pickled in vinegar

. . . as pink as a ham

. . . **quivering** like a blancmange

Or add your own brand-new and completely **scrumptious** foodie simile!

FOODIE facts

In Roald Dahl's stories, readers are sometimes told exactly what characters are eating or drinking. These **delumptious** or **disgustive** clues reveal background detail about the characters and how they live, helping us to get to know them better.

> *The only meals they could afford were bread and margarine for breakfast, boiled potatoes and cabbage for lunch, and cabbage soup for supper. Sundays were a bit better. They all looked forward to Sundays because then, although they had exactly the same, everyone was allowed a second helping.*
> — CHARLIE AND THE CHOCOLATE FACTORY

These foodie facts show that Charlie Bucket and his family eat this bland, boring and very cheap food because they have so little money.

It all started on a blazing hot day in the middle of summer.
Aunt Sponge, Aunt Spiker and James were all out in the
garden. James had been put to work, as usual. This time he was
chopping wood for the kitchen stove. Aunt Sponge and Aunt
Spiker were sitting comfortably in deck-chairs near by, sipping
tall glasses of fizzy lemonade and watching him to see that he
didn't stop work for one moment.

— JAMES AND THE GIANT PEACH

What sort of aunties would sip
fizzy lemonade while their nephew
chopped wood on a blazing hot day?
Mean, thoughtless, cruel aunties,
that's who. Hmm.

Boggis had three boiled chickens smothered in dumplings, Bunce had six doughnuts filled with disgusting goose-liver paste, and Bean had two gallons of cider.
— FANTASTIC MR FOX

Goodness. These meals appear to be neither **scrumptious**, nor healthy. They sound downright **disgusterous**, in fact. Could Farmer Boggis, Farmer Bunce and Farmer Bean perhaps be **disgusterous** too . . . ?

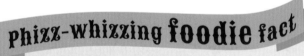

phizz-whizzing foodie fact

A **proverb** is the sort of thing know-it-all adults say. It's a short, well-known saying that might sound a midgy bit annoying, but has a titchy bit of truth or useful advice hidden inside it.

'You are what you eat' is a proverb that means if you eat healthy food, you're likely to be a healthy person too. Do you think Farmer Boggis, Farmer Bunce and Farmer Bean are what they eat . . . ?

Here are more foodie proverbs. Try dropping them into a conversation – ever so casually, of course – and see what effect they have!

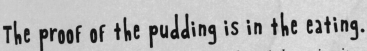

The proof of the pudding is in the eating.

You can only judge how good something is by trying it.

An apple a day keeps the doctor away.

Healthy eating helps to keep you well.

Too many cooks spoil the broth.

If too many people try to do something at the same time, it can go horribly wrong.

37

SCRUMDIDDLYUMPTIOUS Sweets

Real food can be pretty awesome. But when it comes to imaginary food, the sky is truly the limit. It can be as stupendously spectacular as you like. It can even be magical. And it can taste **AMAZING**.

(Remember that you're imagining it. And in your stories, you can imagine whatever you like . . .)

'EATABLE MARSHMALLOW PILLOWS'
'LICKABLE WALLPAPER FOR NURSERIES'
'HOT ICE CREAMS FOR COLD DAYS'

38

'Everlasting Gobstoppers!' cried Mr Wonka proudly. 'They're completely new! I am inventing them for children who are given very little pocket money. You can put an Everlasting Gobstopper in your mouth and you can suck it and suck it and suck it and suck it and it will never get any smaller!'
— CHARLIE AND THE CHOCOLATE FACTORY

I can remember . . . the Electric Fizzcocklers that made every hair on your head stand straight up on end as soon as you popped one into your mouth.
— THE GIRAFFE AND THE PELLY AND ME

A **pun** is a wordy joke. It's funny because words that look or sound alike can actually have different meanings. To begin with, the reader might think that the phrase means one thing. Then, the reader realizes that it does, in fact, mean something else entirely. At this point, they may clutch their sides and cry, '**HA HA HA HA! THAT'S HILARIOUS!**'

Try this one.

Square sweets that look round.

The meaning is crystal clear, right? These are sweets that are square, but actually look as if they are round.

No! Roald Dahl has tricked you.
Here are the sweets.

See? They are . . . square sweets that
look round with their eyes!

Here's another foodie pun from the one and only Willy Wonka:
'Whipped cream isn't whipped cream at all unless it's been
whipped with whips.'

Ha! Obviously, you actually need a whisk to transform cream
into light, fluffy and delightfully **delumptious** whipped
cream. But, if cream were whipped with a whip . . . that would
also be whipped cream! So Mr Wonka is being both clever *and*
silly AT THE SAME TIME.

THREE TOP TIPS FOR INVENTING YOUR OWN PUNS:

1 Read LOTS of joke books and practise the best jokes on
your friends. Don't stop until they groan VERY
LOUDLY. (These jokes will probably be puns.)

2 Look out for newspaper headlines, especially those with
really big letters that cover most of the front page.
Some of these headlines are incredibly clever puns.

3 Keep a list of words that have two meanings, then use the
less obvious meaning whenever you can! (Remember to
smile so that people know you are being hysterically funny.)

HUMAN beans

DON'T PANIC. We haven't heaped human beans on top of toast in a tumbling, tomato-saucy, beany heap. When the BFG says 'human beans', he actually means 'human beings'. This is a **malapropism**.

'Me!' shouted the Giant, his mighty voice making the glass jars rattle on their shelves. 'Me gobbling up human beans! This I never! The others, yes! All the others is gobbling them up every night, but not me!

— THE BFG

42

Some of the characters in Roald Dahl's stories have names that are **GOOD ENOUGH TO EAT**. These names are also very like the characters themselves . . . Is this an incredible coincidence?

NO!

It is very much on purpose. An **aptronym** is a name that is like the person or thing to whom it belongs.

'Daddy!' said Veruca Salt, 'I want a boat like this! I want you to buy me a big pink boiled-sweet boat exactly like Mr Wonka's! And I want lots of Oompa-Loompas to row me about, and I want a chocolate river and I want . . . I want . . .'
— CHARLIE AND THE CHOCOLATE FACTORY

Eating too much salt can make you purse your lips, screw up your eyes and **SHUDDER**. (It's also terribly bad for you.) Reading about thoroughly spoilt Veruca Salt is likely to have the same effect.

Miss Jennifer Honey was a mild and quiet person who never raised her voice . . . she possessed that rare gift for being adored by every small child under her care.
— MATILDA

If all you knew about Miss Honey was her name, you'd already have a good idea that she's **LOVELY**. And it's true! Both Miss Honey AND the honey you spread on toast are sweet and unspeakably pleasant.

The village school for younger children was a bleak brick building called Crunchem Hall Primary School . . .
— MATILDA

The head teacher of Crunchem Hall is the formidable Trunchbull. And what she'd no doubt love to do to her pupils is **CRUNCH 'EM**. (Goodness.)

WHY NOT...?

Make a list of **SCRUMMY** treats and food you completely **DESPISE**. Then use these words to name the heroes and villains in your next story . . .

Amelia Trifle?

Great-aunt Olive?

Russell Sprout?

Mr Guacamole?

45

FRY AND FRIZZLE
simmer and Sizzle

Would you like to make a **scrumptious** and **delumptious** dish? Then you'll need a recipe. You could start with Mrs Twit's recipe for spaghetti.

At one o'clock, she cooked spaghetti for lunch and she mixed the worms in with the spaghetti, but only on her husband's plate.

— THE TWITS

SQUIGGLY SPAGHETTI

YOU WILL NEED:

- spaghetti
- freshly dug worms, preferably big long ones
- tomato sauce
- cheese, grated

WHAT TO DO:

1 Simmer the spaghetti.

2 Drain it.

3 Mix the worms with the spaghetti.

4 Dollop the tomato sauce on top.

5 Sprinkle on cheese.

6 Enjoy this vermicious treat! (But **ONLY** if your name is Mr Twit. If you're **NOT** Mr Twit, leave out the worms.)

There are dillions of **verbs** in recipes. They give terribly useful information to the chef – and they turn a recipe into something **SO** much more exciting than just writing **COOK THIS** and then **COOK THAT** and then, if you really must, **COOK THE OTHER**.

blend sizzle
frizzle fry flambé
mash mince whip
squizzle simmer whizz
toast toss whisk

vermicious *adjective*

Something vermicious is 'worm-like'. This word comes from the Latin word *vermis*, which means, you've guessed it, 'a worm'. And if you think the word looks familiar, you are 100% correct. The vicious and nasty space aliens in *Charlie and the Great Glass Elevator* are called the **VERMICIOUS KNIDS**.

DAHL'S CHICKENS

What's this? Is it an irresistible recipe for roast chicken from the World's Greatest Storyteller himself? No! We have tricked you! Dahl's Chickens is not cooking directions, but a rib-tickling spoonerism instead.

A **spoonerism** has absolutely nothing to do with spoons. It's when a speaker accidentally mixes up the first letters or sounds of two or more words.

'I is reading it hundreds of times,' the BFG said. 'And I is still reading it and teaching new words to myself and how to write them. It is the most scrumdiddlyumptious *story.'*
Sophie took the book out of his hand. 'Nicholas Nickleby,' she read aloud.

'By Dahl's Chickens,' the BFG said.

— THE BFG

The BFG doesn't really mean **DAHL'S CHICKENS** of course.
He means **CHARLES DICKENS**, the world-famous Victorian author!

Meanwhile, can you figure out which delicious yellow
breakfast food the Centipede is talking about when he says
scrambled dregs . . . ?

'I've eaten fresh mudburgers by the greatest cooks there are,

*And **scrambled dregs** and stinkbugs' eggs and hornets stewed in tar,*

And pails of snails and lizards' tails,

And beetles by the jar.

(A beetle is improved by just a splash of vinegar.)'
— JAMES AND THE GIANT PEACH

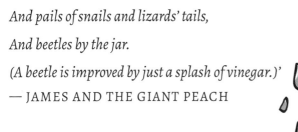

SENSE-ATIONAL FOOD

The merest glimpse of **WONKA'S WHIPPLE-SCRUMPTIOUS FUDGEMALLOW DELIGHT** can be enough to make your mouth water . . .

Charlie tore the wrapper right down the middle . . . and on to his lap, there fell . . . a light-brown creamy-coloured bar of chocolate.
— CHARLIE AND THE CHOCOLATE FACTORY

Yum!

But it's not just the **SIGHT** of food that shows it's likely to be totally toothsome (or really rotsome). If you describe the **TASTE**, **SMELL**, **TOUCH** or **SOUND** of food too, you can make someone's stomach rumble louder than, say, an enormous angry rhinoceros escaping from London Zoo.

SMELL

It was a smell unlike any he had smelled before. It was a brutal and bewitching smell, spicy and staggering, fierce and frenzied, full of wizardry and magic.

— GEORGE'S MARVELLOUS MEDICINE

TASTE

'Every human bean is diddly and different. Some is scrumdiddlyumptious and some is uckyslush.'

— THE BFG

TOUCH

It was as thick around its girth as a perambulator. It was black with white stripes along its length. And it was covered all over with coarse knobbles.

— THE BFG

SOUND

'You mash it and munch it, You chew it and crunch it! It's lovely to hear it go squish!'

— THE ENORMOUS CROCODILE

Psst. For more crunching and squishing, turn over the page!

Some letters sound brittle and hard, like the cr– at the beginning of **crunch**. (Or crrrunch, if you're The Grand High Witch.) Meanwhile, other letters are softer and squidgier, like the sq– at the beginning of **squish**.

The ingredients for Formula 86 Delayed Action Mouse-Maker sound as if they'll be awfully hard to chew.

'So you mix in the egg,' *The Grand High Witch went on,*
'*and vun after the other you also mix in the following*
items: the claw of a crrrabcrrruncher, the beak of a
blabbersnitch, the snout of a grrrobblesqvirt and the
tongue of a catsprrringer.'
— THE WITCHES

Phonaesthesia is the word used to describe how certain groups of letters remind us of certain things.

This vegittible doesn't sound particularly appetizing either.

'So this is the **filthing rotsome glubbage** you is eating!' boomed the Bloodbottler, holding up the partly eaten **snozzcumber**.

— THE BFG

'Is you having any more of this **delunctious grubble** *in your cupboard, Majester?'*
— THE BFG

Delunctious is a blend, which is a mixture of two words. Here, the beginning of delicious and unctious* have been stuck together to create a brand new word. It means tasty or delicious.

* This is VERY like the word unctuous, an adjective that can be used to describe wonderfully thick, gloopy cream.

Grubble is the BFG's own word for grub – or food!

Swobbling is when a giant swallows and gobbles a human bean whole. (Try to avoid this.)

Delumptious – another of the BFG's favourite adjectives – is a blend of delicious and scrumptious.

54

FOOD, FOOD, EVERYWHERE!

In some of Roald Dahl's stories, food is **ALL AROUND**.

Inside The Chocolate Room, Charlie Bucket discovers that **EVERYTHING** is edible. Even the grass can be nibbled!

'The grass you are standing on, my dear little ones, is made of a new kind of soft, minty sugar that I've just invented! I call it swudge! Try a blade! Please do! It's delectable!'
— CHARLIE AND THE CHOCOLATE FACTORY

Willy Wonka's shining, sparkling, glistening pink boat was made by hollowing out an enormous boiled sweet.

A steamy mist was rising up now from the great warm chocolate river, and out of the mist there appeared suddenly a most fantastic pink boat . . . 'This is my private yacht!' cried Mr Wonka, beaming with pleasure. 'I made her by hollowing out an enormous boiled sweet!'
— CHARLIE AND THE CHOCOLATE FACTORY

James Henry Trotter lives, flies and floats inside a giant peach!

The tunnel was damp and murky, and all around him there was the curious bittersweet smell of fresh peach. The floor was soggy under his knees, the walls were wet and sticky, and peach juice was dripping from the ceiling. James opened his mouth and caught some of it on his tongue. It tasted delicious.

— JAMES AND THE GIANT PEACH

This is something you could do too. How about setting a story on a planet made of cheese? Or what if your characters had to cross a sticky syrup swamp and climb a marzipan mountain?

They passed a yellow door on which it said:
STOREROOM NUMBER 77 – ALL THE BEANS,
CACAO BEANS, COFFEE BEANS, JELLY BEANS,
AND HAS BEANS.
'Has beans?' cried Violet Beauregarde.
'You're one yourself!' said Mr Wonka.
— CHARLIE AND THE CHOCOLATE FACTORY

What IS a *has bean*? Is it the name for a baked
bean that has been cooked for so long that it
takes a hammer and chisel to ping it out of the
saucepan? We're afraid not. It isn't even a terribly
funny malapropism. This is . . . wait for it . . . one of
Mr Willy Wonka's puns. IT'S A JOKE.

Has beans and **has-beens** are **homophones** – words that
are pronounced the same, but have different meanings or
spellings. In this case, they have different meanings AND
spellings.

However, if you really must be rude, here are more foodie insults:

'You miserable old mackerel!' said Grandma Georgina, sailing past him.
— CHARLIE AND THE GREAT GLASS ELEVATOR

'that grizzly old grunion of a grandma'
—GEORGE'S MARVELLOUS MEDICINE

A grunion is NOT a misspelling of onion. It is actually the name of a small thin fish found in California.

When the first letters of words next to or near each other start with the same letter, this is called **alliteration**.

Try it yourself! Pick a type of food and then add adjectives that start with the same letter. For example, **fabulous fizzy frobscottle!**

DELUMPTIOUS drinks

If you've read Roald Dahl's stories, you'll already know that two of his most famous drinks start with an F. They are also fizzy, which starts with an F, too. (What are the chances?!) Here they are.

FIZZY LIFTING DRINKS

'They fill you with bubbles, and the bubbles are full of a special kind of gas, and this gas is so terrifically lifting that it lifts you right off the ground just like a balloon . . .'

— CHARLIE AND THE CHOCOLATE FACTORY

Psst. They make you **BURP**. (Goodness.)

FROBSCOTTLE

It was sweet and refreshing. It tasted of vanilla and cream, with just the faintest trace of raspberries on the edge of the flavour.

— THE BFG

Psst. They make you **WHIZZPOP**. (Gosh.)

Which one would YOU rather drink? (If you can't choose, invent your own fabulous new drink.)

rhyme *verb*

Words that rhyme have the same sound as each other. For example, frobscottle rhymes with: bluebottle, mottle, wattle and axolotl – a type of Mexican salamander. Its name comes from a language called Nahuatl, in which atl means 'water' and xolotl means 'servant'.

AND FINALLY...

Nooooooo. You've reached the last page of this **SCRUMPTIOUS** – and also **GROBSWITCHY** – book! The feasts have been eaten. Every last crumb of food has been nibbled and gobbled, chomped and chewed. All the frobscottle has been slurped. What will you do now?!

DO NOT WORRY. Roald Dahl wrote about all sorts of other things, too – such as **WITCHES** and **GIANTS** and **ELEVATORS** and **CROCODILES** and **MISCHIEF**.

You can find all of these and **DILLIONS** more in the whoppsy-whiffling *Oxford Roald Dahl Thesaurus* . . .

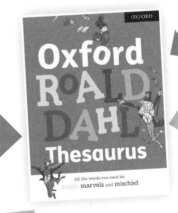

. . . and of course in the splendiferous stories and poems of ROALD DAHL.